AIDING OLDER ADULTS WITH MEMORY COMPLAINTS

Forrest Scogin, PhD
University of Alabama

Mark Prohaska, MS
University of Alabama

Professional Resource Press
Sarasota, Florida

Published by
Professional Resource Press
(An imprint of the Professional Resource Exchange, Inc.)
Post Office Box 15560
Sarasota, FL 34277-1560

Printed in the United States of America

The editorial reviewer for this book was Terry Proeger, PhD, the copy editor was Patricia Hammond, the managing editor was Debra Fink, the production coordinator was Laurie Girsch, and the cover designer was Bill Tabler.

Library of Congress Cataloging-in-Publication Data

Scogin, Forrest Ray.
    Aiding older adults with memory complaints / Forrest Scogin, Mark Prohaska.
        p.   cm. -- (Practitioner's resource series)
    Includes bibliographical references.
    ISBN 0-943158-92-3
    1. Memory disorders in old age. I. Prohaska, Mark. date.
II. Title. III. Series.
        [DNLM: 1. Memory Disorders--in old age. 2. Memory Disorders--therapy. WM 173.7 S422a 1993]
RC394.M46S36   1993
618.97'684--dc20
DNLM/DLC
for Library of Congress   93-13672
                                                            CIP

DEDICATION

To my wife, children, and parents, thanks.

F. Scogin

To my wife, Cynthia,
whose love and support has made an
immeasurable contribution to all my pursuits.

M. Prohaska

PREFACE TO THE SERIES

As a publisher of books, cassettes, and continuing education programs, the Professional Resource Press and Professional Resource Exchange, Inc. strive to provide mental health professionals with highly applied resources that can be used to enhance clinical skills and expand practical knowledge.

All the titles in the *Practitioner's Resource Series* are designed to provide important new information on topics of vital concern to psychologists, clinical social workers, marriage and family therapists, psychiatrists, and other mental health professionals.

Although the focus and content of each book in this series will be quite different, there will be notable similarities:

1. Each title in the series will address a timely topic of critical clinical importance.

2. The target audience for each title will be practicing mental health professionals. Our authors were chosen for their ability to provide concrete "how-to-do-it" guidance to colleagues who are trying to increase their competence in dealing with complex clinical problems.

3. The information provided in these books will represent "state-of-the-art" information and techniques derived from both clinical experience and empirical research. Each of these guide books will include references and resources for those who wish to pursue more advanced study of the discussed topic.

4. The authors will provide numerous case studies, specific recommendations for practice, and the types of "nitty-gritty" details that clinicians need before they can incorporate new concepts and procedures into their practices.

We feel that one of the unique assets of the Professional Resource Press is that all of its editorial decisions are made by mental health professionals. The publisher, all editorial consultants, and all reviewers are practicing psychologists, marriage and family therapists, clinical social workers, and psychiatrists.

If there are other topics you would like to see addressed in this series, please let me know.

Lawrence G. Ritt, Publisher

ABSTRACT

Despite the increasing need for medical and mental health services to older adults, most clinicians have little or no specialized training in geriatrics or gerontology. One of the most common presenting complaints expressed by older clients is poor or failing memory. Research (Lowenstein et al., 1967) indicates that over 50% of those over the age of 60 report experiencing serious memory problems.

This guide describes how memory assessment and memory training can be integrated into the treatment of older adults by nongerontologically trained professionals. It also reviews the evidence on memory change with age, the nature and frequency of memory complaints, studies of various types of memory training with elders, the limitations of such training, and directions for future research. Although this book focuses on ways to provide comprehensive and multimodal services to older adults who complain of memory difficulties, it is not intended to serve as a treatise on the differential diagnosis of pathological and nonpathological memory changes with aging since that topic is comprehensively discussed in other books and is well beyond the scope of this presentation.

TABLE OF CONTENTS

AIDING OLDER
ADULTS WITH
MEMORY COMPLAINTS

INTRODUCTION

As our population ages, clinicians will be more frequently called upon to provide services to older adults. In most cases, the practitioner will have had little or no specialized training in geriatrics or gerontology. The purpose of this book is to prepare the nongerontologically trained professional for a presenting complaint that will occur with regularity in work with older adults: poor or failing memory. It is not the purpose of this work to tackle the problem of differentiating pathological from nonpathological memory change with aging, as this is a topic well covered in other sources and beyond the scope of this presentation. Instead, this presentation will focus upon the older adult in treatment who complains of memory difficulties and the practitioner who wishes to provide a comprehensive and multimodal intervention program. We will begin by reviewing some of the evidence on memory changes with age, the nature and frequency of memory complaints among older adults, and the studies of various types of memory training with elders. We will then describe how memory training can be integrated into work with older adults, discuss the limitations of such training, and close with directions for future research.

MEMORY PERFORMANCE AND AGING

There exists a common belief that memory loss and aging go hand in hand. Most of us know, or have heard of, an older relative living in an institution who cannot remember things as well as he or she once did. Sometimes he or she is able to recall specific events from childhood but can no longer recognize members of the family. This relative, unfortunately, has come to represent the stereotype in our society of what happens to our memory as we age. This stereotype suggests that we will all eventually lose our capacity to remember; that it is just a matter of time. It is no wonder that lapses in memory among older adults take on a whole new meaning - "It's starting to happen to me!"

One of the factors contributing to the stereotype of memory and aging is that older adults do complain more about their memory. A study by Lowenthal et al. (1967) indicated that 50% of subjects over the age of 60, and 66% of those over the age of 75, reported experiencing serious memory problems. In our experience, typical complaints include problems remembering names, dates, phone numbers, appointments, material that has just been read, where something has been put, and what one has gone to the store to buy. Other common memory problems include losing the thread of thought in conversation and a decreased ability to remember both recent and remote events.

Older adults complain more about their memory, but these complaints are often not reflective of actual memory performance. Although these complaints are assumed to reflect an actual decline in memory ability, in reality they may reflect stereotyped beliefs about memory and aging (attributing common memory lapses to the aging process) or be associated with depression (which is highly correlated with memory complaint - a topic to be discussed later). With these alternative explanations available to account for memory complaints, it is important to have a good understanding of expected age changes as they relate to memory. If we assert that inevitable impairment of memory with aging is a myth, the question remains: "What are the facts about the expected changes in memory associated with normal aging?" Will our memory decline and, if so, how much? More importantly, if it does decline, what can be done about it?

Research examining age differences in actual memory performance indicates that the picture is not as grim as most believe. Although some changes in memory functioning occur with age, there does not appear to be a global decline in memory with normal aging. Although an acute or chronic organic brain syndrome often produces marked deficits in memory, the actual changes in memory that occur with normal aging are rather mild. In fact, the deficits that come with normal aging appear to be restricted to rather specific encoding and retrieval processes that tend to be accessible to intervention (Poon, 1985). It is not that the capacity to remember is lost with age, rather, it seems that less efficient encoding and retrieving of to-be-recalled information is evidenced. Fortunately, there are several tested techniques for improving the efficiency of processing information into storage and retrieval systems. The problem is that because objective memory performance and subjective appraisal of memory ability are not always highly correlated, restoring the memory efficiency of older adults to the point that their memory is functioning quite well may not provide relief from memory concerns. It is therefore important also to educate clients about how memory works and to outline the changes in memory that occur with normal aging. In this way, one can attack misperceptions and misattributions regarding memory.

The changes that occur in memory can be understood within a number of theoretical contexts. For ease of presentation, we use the information-processing model of memory which posits the presence of sensory, primary, secondary, and tertiary memory. Each of these will be discussed briefly, and the evidence of age-related changes examined. This review draws heavily upon more extensive reviews by Craik (1977) and Hultsch and Dixon (1990).

SENSORY MEMORY

Sensory memory is hypothesized to consist of a brief storage system for information held just long enough to provide an opportunity to attend to it. If not attended to, this information is quickly lost as it is replaced by new incoming stimuli. A way to demonstrate this type of memory to a client is to casually drop a small object during conversation and then after a few moments ask whether they noticed the sound that it had made. If they had, then the sound had made its way into sensory store, and had been attended to. If they had not noticed the sound, then the stimulus had not been attended to, and had been quickly replaced by other stimuli - perhaps the sound of your voice as you conversed. It is clear that a deficit in sensory memory would have a profound impact on memory performance and complaints, for if information never made it through sensory memory, it would be neither attended to nor remembered.

Although it is true there is some decline in sensory abilities (e.g., vision, hearing) with aging, research has shown only small age differences in sensory memory when these changes are taken into consideration (Kaszniak, Poon, & Riege, 1986). For example, Cerella and Poon (1981) found only slight age differences in iconic memory (a very brief image that remains after exposure to a stimulus) when differences in visual function were eliminated.

PRIMARY MEMORY

Once attended to, information is thought to be transferred from sensory memory to primary memory. Primary memory is that portion of the information processing system that attends to, controls, and assimilates information prior to storage in secondary memory. Primary memory can best be thought of in terms of a limited "working memory" that will hold about seven pieces of information. Deficits in primary memory would interrupt the storage process and not allow even short-term recall of information. For example, a phone number looked up in the phone book could not be remembered from the time of looking it up to the time of dialing were primary memory not functioning properly. Primary memory then involves the ability to retain information in memory while actually attending to it.

Research has shown that in tasks of primary memory such as free recall of word lists and digit span, performance remains fairly stable and efficient with age when the items have been properly perceived and when the amount of information is within the limits of primary store (Craik, 1977). The most significant change in primary memory functioning with aging is a slowing in the rate of retrieval from primary storage (Craik, 1977).

4

SECONDARY MEMORY

After information enters the sensory system and is attended to, if it is to be retained, it must enter the secondary memory store. Secondary memory is that portion of memory that stores information on a longer term basis. Information that can be retrieved without constant rehearsal can be said to have entered secondary memory. It is in this type of memory that the greatest evidence for age-related differences exists. In tasks that require learning and later recall of information, older adults tend to do worse than younger adults, especially when the information to be remembered exceeds the limits of primary memory. Specifically, research suggests that older adults do less well on tasks that require elaborate processing, organization of information, and visual elaboration of stimuli (Eysenck, 1974; Poon, 1985). In tasks that insure proper encoding of material, however, the rates of forgetting information are virtually identical for younger and older adults. Therefore, it appears that the differences in secondary memory are due to a deficit in the encoding and retrieval strategies used by older adults and not to a lack of ability to store information (Kaszniak et al., 1986).

TERTIARY MEMORY

Tertiary memory can be thought of in terms of a long-term memory store where all of our experiences, language, familiar information, and so on are stored. A review of the literature on retrieval of information from tertiary memory by Erber (1981) found no significant age differences between older and younger adults in performance.

In summary, the evidence suggests that in normal aging there is little decline in our ability to perceive information in the environment, attend to it, store information in secondary memory, or retrieve information from tertiary memory. It does appear, however, that with aging one tends to become less efficient at encoding information in secondary memory in a way that allows easy access or retrieval. The more elaborate the encoding required to store information, the more difficulty older adults tend to have in retrieval. Thus, it is plausible that it is not memory capacity, but rather memory efficiency, that declines with age.

MEMORY COMPLAINTS

Given this information, a logical approach to working with older clients with memory complaints would be to teach more efficient and effective encoding and retrieval strategies. Possessing more efficient memory strategies should theoretically result in fewer memory failures, fewer embarrassments, and fewer complaints. Unfortunately, it appears that even though this approach may improve actual memory performance, it may do relatively little to alleviate memory complaints. For example, in a memory training study with older adults, Scogin, Storandt, and Lott (1985) found that even though memory performance improved with training in specific memory enhancement techniques, complaints about memory remained at pretraining levels. This suggests that memory complaints and memory performance are not isomorphic.

A large body of research has focused on how accurate older adults are in assessing their memory. Studies generally find that most older adults are fairly accurate in assessing their memories. In a study of subjects who were not selected on the basis of having memory complaints, Zelinski, Gilewski, and Thompson (1980) found that community-dwelling older adults were very accurate in their appraisal of their memory, and were even somewhat more accurate than were younger adults. It is important to note, however, that studies involving groups of older adults who are more likely to appear in a clinician's office have not replicated these findings. Specifically, older adults with memory complaints, and those who are depressed, have been shown to be less accurate in their appraisal of their memory performance.

In a study of older adults with memory complaints, Zarit, Cole, and Guider (1981) found that the correlation between memory complaints and memory performance was not significant. In comparing older subjects with and without memory complaints, Scogin (1985) found that those with fewer memory complaints appraised their memory performance more accurately than adults with greater concerns about their memory. Therefore, it may frequently be the case that the actual memory performance of older adults with memory complaints is quite good, but complaints still exist due to inaccurate beliefs and expectations about cognitive abilities (Scogin, 1985; Zarit, Cole, & Guider, 1981).

MEMORY COMPLAINTS AND DEPRESSION

Depression appears to play a role in both the accuracy of memory assessment and the number of memory complaints. Researchers have found that depression is positively associated with memory complaints. Specifically, increased levels of depression have been shown to be accompanied by more complaints about memory performance (Kahn et al., 1975; Popkin et al., 1982). There is evidence to suggest that the depressive's complaints about memory may be independent of memory performance, and that a depressive's memory performance may not be objectively different from others in spite of the high number of memory complaints (Kahn et al., 1975; O'Hara et al., 1986). Further evidence of the link between memory complaints and depression comes from the finding that as depression decreases over time, so do complaints about memory (Zarit, Cole, & Guider, 1981; Zarit, Gallagher, & Kramer, 1981). In a study comparing depressed and nondepressed older adults, Popkin et al. (1982) found that although memory performance was the same in depressed and nondepressed groups, the depressed group had significantly more memory complaints. It was also found that as the levels of depression decreased in the depressed group, the differences in memory complaints disappeared.

Zarit (1980) hypothesized that stereotypes about getting older may play a role in the inaccuracy of memory assessment by some older adults. Because of inaccurate beliefs, normal instances of memory lapses may be misinterpreted as evidence of a serious memory disturbance. If this is the case, it makes sense that the problem would be compounded with depressed clients. Because depressives tend to interpret events in more negative ways, they may also be misinterpreting memory failures more negatively than is actually warranted (Zarit, 1980).

In summary, most older adults are accurate in assessing their memory functioning. Those with numerous memory complaints or depression, on the other hand, appear to be less reliable judges of their memory performance. This poses an obvious dilemma for the clinician. As Zarit (1980) points out, many diagnostic and treatment decisions for older patients are based on the quality and quantity of memory complaints. Research, however, suggests that the complaints of those most likely to seek treatment may not correspond to objective cognitive functioning. Therefore, a careful objective assessment of memory performance should be conducted prior to any treatment decisions. Clearly, any intervention for memory complaints must address both memory functioning and beliefs and expectations concerning cognitive abilities (Scogin, 1985).

MEMORY ASSESSMENT

This book is not intended to be a primer on memory assessment of the older adult, as this would be well beyond its scope. For readers interested in a more detailed treatment of this topic, we recommend the *Handbook for Clinical Memory Assessment of Older Adults* edited by Poon (1986). However, it is important that clinicians working with older adults with memory complaints have sufficient background in assessment to enable them to accurately evaluate the severity and, if possible, the causes of clients' difficulties. For simplicity, it is useful to think of the two major domains of assessment as the areas of objective and subjective memory functioning. As noted earlier, there tends not to be a strong correlation between these two domains, especially among older adults likely to be seen by service providers. Consequently, assessment is necessary in order to determine the focus of treatment or whether referral to a more appropriate provider is indicated. For example, one might structure an intervention quite differently for a client with high levels of memory complaint who performs quite well on objective performance indices than for a client who performs rather poorly on objective measures but displays only moderate levels of complaint. Thus, as in most areas of clinical practice, assessment becomes a key to proper intervention.

ASSESSMENT OF OBJECTIVE MEMORY FUNCTIONING

The assessment of objective memory and cognitive functioning as it relates to memory training can be conceptualized as a multistage procedure. The first stage is a gross appraisal of the client's cognitive functioning and can be summarized by the question, "Is this individual evidencing dementia or normal age-related memory impairments?" In some cases, this diagnostic question is easily answered, for example, when the client is grossly impaired. More frequently, the client will present a more difficult differential diagnostic question. Many participants in our memory training research program have quite a few specific complaints about their memory functioning and note the changes they have experienced in such functions as they have grown older. The assessment issue becomes one of determining whether this person has the capacity to profit from a memory training program. A good initial assessment involves the administration of a brief screening instrument such as the Mental Status Questionnaire (Kahn et al., 1960) or the Mini-Mental State (M. F. Folstein, S. E. Folstein, & McHugh, 1975). Persons scoring below the cutoff indicative of substantial impairment are in most cases poor candidates for the memory training procedures (lower scores on these instruments are indicative of impairment). Individuals complaining of memory difficulties who score poorly on these brief screening instruments should be evaluated more extensively for the presence of dementia.

Individuals who pass screening on such instruments are then subjected to more detailed assessment of their memory functioning. Consistent with the recommendations of Crook et al. (1986), a standardized measure of memory performance that has adequate normative data, such as the Wechsler Memory Scale-Revised (WMS-R; Wechsler, 1987), can be used to determine the client's relative memory functioning. Crook et al. (1986) proposed a research diagnosis they termed age-associated memory impairment (AAMI) that is relevant to this discussion. The inclusion and exclusion criteria are reproduced here. Clients evidencing AAMI as defined by these authors are candidates for memory training.

1. Inclusion criteria
   a. Males and females at least 50 years of age.
   b. Complaints of memory loss reflected in such everyday problems as difficulty remembering names of individuals following introduction, misplacing objects, difficulty remembering multiple items to be purchased or multiple tasks to be performed, remembering telephone numbers or zip codes, and difficulty recalling information quickly or following distraction. Onset of memory loss must be de-

scribed as *gradual,* without sudden worsening in recent months.

c. Memory test performance that is at least 1 standard deviation below the mean established for young adults on a standardized test of secondary memory (recent memory) with adequate normative data.

d. Evidence of adequate intellectual functioning as determined by a scaled score of at least 9 (raw score of at least 32) on the Vocabulary subtest of the Wechsler Adult Intelligence Scale-R (WAIS-R; Wechsler, 1981).

e. Absence of dementia as determined by a score of 24 or higher on the Mini-Mental State (M. F. Folstein et al., 1975).

2. Exclusion criteria

a. Evidence of delirium, confusion, or other disturbances of consciousness.

b. Any neurologic disorder that could produce cognitive deterioration as determined by history and clinical neurological examination. Such disorders include Alzheimer's disease, Parkinson's disease, stroke, intracranial hemorrhage, local brain lesions including tumors, and normal pressure hydrocephalus.

c. History of any infective or inflammatory brain disease including those of viral, fungal, or syphilitic etiologies.

d. Evidence of significant cerebral vascular pathology as determined by a Hachinski Ischemia Score (Rosen et al., 1980) of 4 or more, or by neuroradiologic examination.

e. History of repeated minor head injury (e.g., in boxing) or single injury resulting in a period of unconsciousness for 1 hour or more.

f. Current psychiatric diagnosis according to *DSM-III-R* (American Psychiatric Association, 1987) criteria of depression, mania, or any major psychiatric disorder.

g. Current diagnosis or history of alcoholism or drug dependence.

h. Evidence of depression as determined by a Hamilton Depression Rating Scale (Hamilton, 1967) score of 13 or more.

i. Any medical disorder that could produce cognitive deterioration including renal, respiratory, cardiac, and hepatic disease; diabetes mellitus unless well controlled by diet or oral hypoglycemics; endocrine, metabolic, or hematologic disturbances; and malignancy not in remission for more than 2 years. Determination should be based on complete medical history, clinical examination (including electrocardiogram), and appropriate laboratory tests.

j.   Use of any psychotropic drug or any other drug that may significantly affect cognitive function during the month prior to psychometric testing.

In addition to establishing the severity of memory impairment, the assessment of objective memory performance should also be used to determine the types of memory difficulties that may be targeted for training. In our research protocol, we use assessments of memory function with relatively high ecological validity (i.e., tasks with relevance to everyday functioning). For example, participants recall a shopping list, memorize names and faces, and recall a paragraph read to them. Some clients show relatively stable functioning across such tasks, while others show particular decrements on one type of task or another. It is also important to determine as much as possible the *cause* of poor performance. The information-processing paradigm presented earlier that includes encoding, storage, and retrieval stages is useful for this purpose. Older adults often use inefficient encoding strategies as demonstrated by attempts to use rote memory to recall item lists and name-face pairings.

Such observations are consistent with the literature reviewed previously that suggests that older adults tend to spontaneously use less efficient encoding strategies. The work of Buschke is pertinent to this discussion. Buschke (1984) makes a distinction between production deficiencies and memory deficiencies. The former has to do with inefficient processing of information; older adults often demonstrate deficiencies in this domain. A production deficiency leads to poorer memory function but does not necessarily imply that a person is incapable of improved memory performance. From this conceptual framework, poorer memory performance caused by production deficits should be distinguished from true memory deficits evident when the processing of information is optimal. Persons most likely to profit from the sorts of training we provide are those demonstrating production deficits. Indeed, the focus of memory training is the augmentation of production processes. If one can isolate an information-processing inefficiency, then memory training can be targeted more effectively. Also, information gleaned from assessment can in this way be used to provide a rationale to clients for the causes of their difficulties and the direction that intervention efforts may take.

ASSESSMENT OF SUBJECTIVE MEMORY FUNCTIONING

Assessment of objective performance is coupled with assessment of clients' perception of their memory function. Assessment of subjective memory functioning is most readily accomplished by interview and questionnaire administration. Interview questions should be focused on clarifying clients' feelings, attitudes, and beliefs surrounding memory functioning. For example, some clients have somewhat unrealistic expectations of their memory functioning (and in some cases memory training) that can lead to a vigilant, self-critical approach to memory failures. Questions such as "What types of difficulties do you have with your memory," "How do you feel when this difficulty occurs," and "What do you do to try to avoid such difficulties" can provide a great deal of information pertinent to developing an intervention program.

Standardized questionnaire assessment of memory functioning can also provide useful information. We recommend and use the Memory Functioning Questionnaire (MFQ; Gilewski, Zelinski, & Schaie, 1990) and the Metamemory in Adulthood instrument (MIA; Dixon & Hultsch, 1984). The MFQ is a 64-item questionnaire that yields three factors: frequency of failures, perceived seriousness of these failures, and mnemonics/retrospective functioning. Each item is rated on a 7-point Likert scale. Illustrative items are presented in Table 1 (p. 13). Internal consistency estimates for the MFQ range from .82 to .93 using Cronbach's alpha. Test-retest reliabilities over a 3-year period ranged from .22 to .64 (Gilewski & Zelinski, 1986). The authors of this instrument note several advantages relative to other questionnaires. First, the psychometric qualities of the MFQ are well established. Furthermore, the instrument was validated on samples of older adults. Also, scores on the instrument have correlated significantly with memory performance indices among normal older adults.

TABLE 1:   SAMPLE ITEMS FROM GILEWSKI, ZELINSKI,
            AND SCHAIE'S (1990) MEMORY FUNCTIONING
            QUESTIONNAIRE*

Scale	Sample Item
1. General Rating	How would you rate your memory in terms of the kinds of problems you have?
2. Retrospective	How is your memory functioning compared to the way it was 1 year ago?
3. Frequency of Forgetting	How often do these present a problem for you . . . (a) names?
4. Frequency of Forgetting When Reading	As you are reading a novel, how often do you have trouble remembering what you have read . . . (a) in the opening chapters once you have finished the book?
5. Remembering Past Events	How well do you remember things which occurred . . . (a) last month?
6. Seriousness	When you actually forget in these situations, how serious of a problem do you consider the memory failure to be . . . (a) names.
7. Mnemonics	How often do you use these techniques to remind yourself about things . . . (a) keep an appointment book.

---

*Note. Adapted from "The Memory Functioning Questionnaire for Assessment of Memory Complaints in Adulthood and Old Age" by M. J. Gilewski, E. M. Zelinski, and K. W. Schaie, 1990, *Psychology and Aging, 5,* pp. 482-490.

The MIA is a 120-item questionnaire that taps eight dimensions: strategy use, task knowledge, knowledge of memory capacity, perception of age change, activities supportive of memory, anxiety and memory, achievement motivation and memory, and locus of control and memory. Illustrative items are presented in Table 2 (p. 14). Cronbach's alpha ranged from .61 to .91 on seven of the scales, with the activities supportive of memory dimension demonstrating less consistency across three samples. The MIA and MFQ complement each other well in that the MIA tends to focus on personality factors as they relate to memory complaints, while the MFQ tends to focus on the types of memory problems experienced.

It is also recommended that one or both of these questionnaires be completed by a spouse or significant other familiar with the client for purposes of comparison. A recently completed study by Scogin and Rohling (1990) suggests that significant others may be a bit more accurate in appraising the memory performance of older adults than older adults themselves. In this study, higher levels of correspondence between subjective and objective memory performance were found when the rater was a significant other (e.g., spouse, child, friend, etc.) than when the subject rated his or her own memory. An interview with or completion of

---

TABLE 2:   SAMPLE ITEMS FROM DIXON AND HULTSCH'S (1984) METAMEMORY IN ADULTHOOD QUESTIONNAIRE*

<u>Dimension</u>	<u>Sample Item</u>
1. Strategy Use	107. Do you write appointments on a calendar to help you remember them?
2. Task Knowledge	1. For most people, facts that are interesting are easier to remember than facts that are not.
3. Knowledge of Memory Capacity	2. I am good at remembering names.
4. Perception of Age Change	17. The older I get the harder it is to remember things clearly.
5. Activities Supportive of Memory	72. How often do you read newspapers?
6. Anxiety and Memory	9. I find it harder to remember things when I am upset.
7. Achievement Motivation and Memory	69. It's important that I am very accurate when remembering names of people.
8. Locus of Control and Memory	79. Even if I work on it my memory ability will go downhill.

---

*Note. From "The Metamemory in Adulthood (MIA) Instrument" by R. A. Dixon and D. F. Hultsch, 1984, *Psychological Documents, 14*, p. 3. Reprinted by permission.

---

a relevant questionnaire by a significant other can thus potentially provide valuable collateral and/or corroborative information.

ASSESSMENT OF AFFECTIVE STATUS

A final area of assessment concerns the client's affective status. Assessment of affective status is important for several reasons. First, the differentiation between depression-produced memory impairment (sometimes referred to as "pseudodementia") and organic brain disorders is often difficult. Memory impairment related to depression is potentially amenable to memory training, especially memory training augmented with treatment for depression. Second, as noted previously, depression and complaints about memory tend to be related. Thus, a reliable and sensitive measure of depression is integral to treatment planning.

Clinical lore suggests that depressed persons, especially older adults, evidence decrements in memory performance, and there are a number of studies that tend to support this position (e.g., Henry, Weingartner, & Murphy, 1973; Hilbert, Niederehe, & Kahn, 1976). However, other studies report no impairment in memory performance among depressed elders (e.g., Kahn et al., 1975; Popkin et al., 1982). Consequently, researchers such as Niederehe (1986) suggest that an unequivocal statement about the depression-memory impairment linkage cannot be made. Of course, the equivocal nature of the literature tends only to make the psychological assessment of the older adult even more complex.

A number of depression assessment techniques are available for use with the older adult. One instrument frequently used is the Hamilton Rating Scale for Depression (HRSD; Hamilton, 1967), a measure of depression severity. For those more interested in *DSM-III-R* diagnoses, the Schedule for Affective Disorders and Schizophrenia (SADS; Spitzer & Endicott, 1978) is recommended, though the length of this interview is often prohibitive. For self-report measures of depression, either the Geriatric Depression Scale (GDS; Yesavage, Brink, et al., 1983) or the Beck Depression Inventory (BDI; Beck et al., 1961) can be used. Both are relatively brief, reliable, and valid, and demonstrate acceptable sensitivity and specificity. Interestingly, one of the items on the GDS asks respondents "Do you feel you have more prob-

15

lems with memory than most?" The inclusion of this item on a brief instrument designed specifically for geriatric depression attests to the strong link between affective disturbance and memory complaints. Practitioners who are unfamiliar with the special issues encountered in depression assessment with older adults are referred to excellent overviews of this topic by Gallagher (1986) and Yesavage (1986). Clients experiencing clinical levels of depression should be treated or referred accordingly.

Practitioners interested in a more global assessment of mental health through self-report are referred to the Symptoms Checklist (SCL-90; Derogatis, Rickels, & Rock, 1976) or the Brief Symptom Inventory (BSI; Derogatis & Spencer, 1982). These instruments provide age norms and are brief and easily understood by most older adults. Additionally, subscales including depression, anxiety, paranoia, psychoticism, and hostility allow more detailed assessment of particular clusters of symptoms.

The various sources of information make diagnosis in this area rather complicated. Thompson (1980) provided a sequence of decision making when assessing the older adult with memory deficits or memory complaints. If the person complains of memory problems but evidences normal memory performance on objective tests and shows signs of depression, then depression may be the primary contributor to the perceived memory problems. If memory complaints are numerous when memory performance is normal and depression is not apparent, then anxiety may be increasing the complaints. When memory performance and memory complaints are both low and no depression is detected, then neurological dysfunction is more likely. If complaints are high and memory performance is low in the presence of depression, diagnostic status is uncertain. Treatment of depression that results in improved memory performance suggests nonorganic impairment, while treatment for depression that does not result in improved memory performance suggests organic impairment.

COGNITIVE TRAINING IN BRAIN
INJURY AND REHABILITATION PROGRAMS

Memory training is also a service provided to those who have experienced head injury or an insult to the central nervous system that impairs memory function. The work of Butters and colleagues (e.g., Butters et al., 1986; Salmon & Butters, 1987) suggests that the heterogeneity of processes underlying impairments exhibited by differing diagnostic groups makes general statements about memory training practically impossible. For example, individuals exhibiting Korsakoff's syndrome will respond more favorably to certain rehabilitative strategies than will persons exhibiting Huntington's disease. O'Connor and Cermak (1987) catalog several techniques applicable to neuropsychological rehabilitation, including imagery mnemonics and external memory aids. These techniques comprise portions of the memory training program that is presented later in this document. Existing rehabilitation programs stress the importance of careful assessment of cognitive function and the development of a program that addresses deficits while building rehabilitative strategies around preserved memory capacities (Salmon & Butters, 1987). Assessment seems especially important with head-injured persons because the possibility of focal cognitive deficit is greater than with age-associated memory impairment or the dementias. Readers interested in more detailed coverage of these issues are referred to Meier, Benton, and Diller (1987) and Wilson (1987).

One of the major criticisms of memory training with brain-injured persons concerns the applicability of the training to everyday life (O'Connor & Cermak, 1987). For example, the relevancy of rather complicated imagery mnemonics to already impaired individuals is questioned. Similar concerns have been raised about the applicability of memory training for older adults. We can provide no definitive response to these concerns, though it seems in part to be an empirical question. Do participants find the training relevant and applicable? Is everyday as well as laboratory-based memory functioning improved as a result of participation in memory training programs? Answers to these questions await further research; however, we will attempt to share some of the reactions of our memory training participants to the techniques that we have taught as well as some examples of how they were applied in everyday situations.

COMPUTER-ASSISTED MEMORY TRAINING

Another aspect of current memory rehabilitation programs is the use of personal computers. Several advantages of computer-assisted memory rehabilitation are (a) cost/time savings, (b) provision of standard/controlled conditions, (c) flexibility, (d) production of timed responses, (e) patient acceptability, and (f) ease of data analysis (Skilbeck, 1984). Training by the use of personal computers would be a logical extension in work with older adults complaining of memory difficulties, provided that obstacles to access could be removed.

Two studies have investigated the use of computer-assisted memory training with elders. Leirer et al. (1988) explored medication recall training by computer assistance. The participants completed brief training on a specific memory enhancement technique designed to increase medication adherence and were compared to a group receiving more traditional mnemonic training. The results clearly favored the specific medication mnemonic group and lend support to the potential efficacy of computer-assisted memory training.

A second study of computer-assisted memory training was conducted by Finkel and Yesavage (1990). These investigators compared list learning following computer-assisted or traditional group memory training. Subjects were taught the method of loci, a mnemonic technique described later in this text. Finkel and Yesavage found that list recall scores were improved at posttest for the computer-assisted group and, further, that the mean improvement for this group was not significantly different from that evidenced by the traditional training group. This lack of difference in efficacy suggests that computer-assisted training may have potential for some older adults with memory complaints.

THE MEMORY TRAINING PROGRAM

Instruction in the use of mnemonic strategies is the most popular nonpharmacologic approach to improving memory performance in older adults. We have evaluated the effectiveness of both self-taught and group memory training with older adults complaining of memory difficulties. An outline and protocol for these modalities are presented in Table 3 (pp. 20-21). In the memory programs that we have developed and tested, we begin training by providing trainees with an understanding of the information processing model of memory and the changes in memory that can be expected with normal aging within that model. This information helps to dispel the mistaken beliefs about memory that many older adults have and sets the stage for understanding the rationale for the mnemonic techniques that follow. We also point out that older adults tend to forget the same types of information as do younger people, and we stress that these memory lapses are not necessarily indicative of impending dementia. In so doing, we attempt to establish realistic expectations of memory performance and adaptive attributions for the memory lapses that everyone experiences from time to time. Zarit, Cole, and Guider (1981) point out that an important part of any memory training program is screening for severe memory loss associated with senile dementia. Such screening allows trainers to reassure participants that they fall into the category of "normal aging" and facilitates the shift in attributional style that is so important in changing subjective concerns about memory performance.

If memory training is provided in a group setting, the opportunity also exists for participants to share with others their concerns and experiences with memory failures. Feedback from participants in our group programs indicates that this single aspect of the training is what they found to be most reassuring and helpful in dispelling many of their fears. To learn that one is not the only one "in the boat" is reassuring and also tends to reinforce the material presented on normal memory changes.

There is a fairly large body of research suggesting that poor organization of information and the failure to use imagery are related to age differences in memory. Consequently, the most successful techniques for improving the acquisition and retention of information tend to follow two approaches: strategies for better organization of material to be remembered and the use of visual imagery to make associations between material to be remembered and other images that serve as memory cues.

Sanders et al. (1980) found that older adults' spontaneous approach to memorizing a word list tended to be inactive and without strategy, consisting primarily of simply saying the word once to themselves as it was presented. Younger adults, on the other hand, tended to actively rehearse the list as it was presented and to spontaneously organize the list into categories. There is also evidence that older adults are less able to detect or respond to organization within presented stimuli (Rabbitt, 1964) and that older adults present an increasing deficit in recalling nonsense syllables

19

**TABLE 3:   GROUP AND SELF-TAUGHT
MEMORY TRAINING PROTOCOLS**

Following are the protocol and outline for the group and self-taught memory training programs, respectively, that have been evaluated in our research.

<u>Group Memory Training Protocol</u>

Session One

    I.   Overview and Orientation (10 minutes)
    II.   Introduction of Group Members (10 minutes)
    III.   Overview of Memory and Aging (30 minutes)
    IV.   Break (10 minutes)
    V.   Technique #1: Physical Reminders (40 minutes)
    VI.   Homework Assignments and Review (20 minutes)

Session Two

    I.   Review of Session One (5 minutes)
    II.   Discuss Homework Assignments (20 minutes)
    III.   Technique #2: Chunking (25 minutes)
    IV.   Break (10 minutes)
    V.   Technique #3: Categorization (25 minutes)
    VI.   Introduction to Imagery and Imagery Exercise (15 minutes)
    VII. Homework Assignments and Review (20 minutes)

Session Three

    I.   Review of Sessions One and Two (10 minutes)
    II.   Discuss Homework Assignments (10 minutes)
    III.   Technique #4: Novel Interacting Images (40 minutes)
    IV.   Break (10 minutes)
    V.   Technique #5: Method of Loci (40 minutes)
    VI.   Homework Assignments and Review (10 minutes)

Session Four

    I.   Discuss Homework Assignments (20 minutes)
    II.   Review Memory and Aging (10 minutes)

Session Four (Continued)

  III.   Review of Technique #1: Physical Reminders (10 minutes)
  IV.   Review of Technique #2: Chunking (10 minutes)
   V.   Break (10 minutes)
  VI.   Review of Technique #3: Categorization (10 minutes)
  VII.   Review of Technique #4: Novel Interacting Images (10 minutes)
VIII.   Review of Technique #5: Method of Loci (10 minutes)
  IX.   Feedback from Group Members (30 minutes)

Self-Taught Memory Training Outline

Day	_Subject_
1	Introduction
2	Physical Reminders I
3	Physical Reminders II
4	Physical Reminders III
5	Chunking and Categorization
6	Categorization
7	Review of Chunking and Categorization
8	Review of Physical Reminders, Chunking, and Categorization
9	Preparation for Imagery I
10	Preparation for Imagery II
11	The Method of Loci I
12	The Method of Loci II
13	The Method of Loci III
14	The Method of Loci IV
15	The Method of Loci V
16	Names and Faces I
17	Names and Faces II
18	Names and Faces III
19	Names and Faces IV
20	Names and Faces V
21	Review of the Method of Loci and Names and Faces
22	Other Uses of Imagery I
23	Other Uses of Imagery II
24	Review of the Manual

compared to younger adults as the stimuli become more amenable to organization. This again reflects a deficit in the use of organizational strategies among older adults.

Imagery skills also tend to be less frequently used by older groups to aid recall. Evidence suggests that older adults are less likely than younger adults to use visual imagery as a memory strategy (Camp, Markley, & Kramer, 1983; Hulicka & Grossman, 1967) and tend not to use a visual imagery mnemonic technique that they have learned without explicit prompting (Robertson-Tchabo, Hausman, & Arenberg, 1976). An interesting finding in some studies is that when organizational and imagery techniques are used in memory tasks, older adults tend to perform as well as younger adults (Laurence, 1967; Yesavage, 1985). This finding offers strong support for the notion of teaching mnemonic strategies to older adults experiencing age-related memory problems.

Of the numerous types of organizational and visual mnemonic strategies available, four stand out in the literature with older adults and show the greatest promise for improving memory performance (Robertson-Tchabo et al., 1976; Yesavage, Rose, & Bower, 1983; Zarit, Cole, & Guider, 1981; Zarit, Gallagher, & Kramer, 1981). Two of these techniques, categorization and chunking, involve improving the organization of information to be remembered. The other two techniques, the method of loci and novel interacting images, involve the use of imagery. Another technique that we discuss in our training is the use of physical reminders as memory cues. Although this technique is difficult to study in the laboratory, common sense and feedback from participants in our studies suggest that it is a worthwhile and useful approach to handling some common memory complaints. Each of these techniques will be discussed in sufficient depth to allow their application, and we will attempt to illustrate some of the ways that our memory training participants have incorporated these techniques into their daily lives.

ORGANIZATIONAL TECHNIQUES

Categorization. Categorization is the first of two mnemonic techniques that attempt to improve the organization of material that is to be remembered. This technique is applicable to remembering lists of items that can be grouped into categories based on similarities. As mentioned earlier, primary memory, which is the rehearsal area of memory for the transfer of information into secondary store, is hypothesized to have a limit of about seven pieces of information. If one were to try to remember a list of nine words in a free-recall task, great difficulty would be experienced in trying to hold them in primary memory long enough to process them into secondary store because the limits of the primary store would have been exceeded. Categorization, however, provides a means of holding all nine pieces of information in primary storage by breaking down the information into categories, each of which contains a manageable number of items to be remembered. As long as the number of categories is within the limits of primary memory, information can be efficiently encoded for later retrieval.

To illustrate how categorization can work, consider the following list of nine items:

> Napkins
> Oranges
> Pepper
> Plums
> Toilet Paper
> Salt
> Bananas
> Ginger
> Paper Towels

As previously mentioned, a strategy commonly used by older adults would be merely to repeat these words as they were presented and then attempt to recall them (Sanders et al., 1980). This approach is doomed to failure because the amount of information is too large to rehearse and maintain in primary storage, and merely saying the word once will not be sufficient for transfer to and retrieval from secondary memory.

Categorization, on the other hand, suggests organizing the information into categories based on shared similarities. The items in this example easily fit into three categories: paper products, spices, and fruits, each of which contains three items. Rehearsing and storing these three categories, and the three items within each category, is easier than trying to rehearse the nine items separately. The categorized organization would appear as follows:

1. Paper Products
   a. Napkins
   b. Toilet Paper
   c. Paper Towels
2. Spices
   a. Pepper
   b. Salt
   c. Ginger
3. Fruits
   a. Oranges
   b. Plums
   c. Bananas

To transfer this information into secondary storage, rehearsal of four sets of information is needed: the list of the three categories, and the items found within each category. This could be accomplished by saying "This list consists of three categories - paper products (which consists of napkins, toilet paper, and paper towels), spices (which consists of pepper, salt, and ginger), and fruits (consisting of oranges, plums, and bananas)." The retrieval process involves going back through this organization process by recalling first the category, and then the items within the category. Because this is the way the information was encoded, retrieval is facilitated. The categories serve as a memory cue to the items within each category, which come to mind in the fashion rehearsed.

Our training participants typically report that this technique is one of their favorites and one that they find themselves using frequently on a day-to-day basis. It is easy to demonstrate its effectiveness in an exercise during training, and most people are able to attain 100% recall of lists containing 15 to 20 words with very little practice time.

The other reason that this technique is popular is that it is applicable to everyday memory tasks. By far the most common use of this technique is for trips to the grocery store. Many participants have found that rather than categorizing their shopping items by similarity, it is more helpful to categorize them by location in the supermarket. For example, all of the items in aisle one are grouped together, then the items in the frozen food aisle, and so on. This not only makes the list easy to remember, but also organizes their trip through the store and cuts down on unnecessary backtracking to pick up items that they missed the first time around. This technique has been applied to other lists that could be broken down into categories, such as a lengthy errand list or a list of relatives who would be at a reunion. The relatives would be categorized by the first letter of their name (i.e., all of the As, then the Bs, etc.).

This technique was also used by one of our participants who was having trouble remembering what he had read in the newspaper. This upset him because he liked to discuss current events with his friends, and he too often forgot the details of what he had read. He solved this problem by categorizing each article of interest using categories like who, what, when, where, how, and so on. During his discussions, he found that he could recall what was to him an astonishing amount of detail about the topics under discussion. Another training participant found the technique helpful in memorizing passages from the Bible. Although we never fully understood the complex system of categorization that was used to accomplish this, the point was clearly made that this is a versatile technique that can, with a little imagination, be applied to a wide variety of situations.

Research on this technique with older adults has yielded promising results. Laurence (1967) provided young and elderly groups with a list of 36 words in a free recall task. These words fit into six categories: flowers, trees, birds, formations of nature, vegetables, and countries. Although younger subjects recalled significantly more information than the older group in a free recall condition, this age difference disappeared when the categories applicable to the word list were presented for use during the recall period. Laurence concluded that categories can provide an effective cue-at-recall strategy to reduce the problems that older adults experience in the recall of information.

Schmitt, Martin, and Sanders (1981) compared groups receiving categorization instructions with a group instructed to actively rehearse a list of words and a control group told only to remember the list. They found that the group that used categorization showed the best recall and the highest levels of category organization compared to the other two groups. They concluded that although older adults have the requisite abilities to use effective strategies, they demonstrate a deficiency in generating them on their own. Their ability to use strategies such as categorization, however, demonstrates the utility of training older adults in their use.

Chunking. Chunking, the second organizational technique, is closely related to categorization. This technique is particularly appropriate for remembering numbers. If there is a need to remember a telephone number consisting of seven numbers, the full capacity of primary memory must be used for rehearsal in an attempt to get it into secondary store for later recall. However, if there is a need to remember a social security number consisting of nine numbers, or a phone number just given on television to call about insurance for senior citizens consisting of 11 numbers, then the task is greater than the limits of primary memory will allow.

Chunking is a method that increases the capacity of secondary memory by reducing the amount of information to be remembered by organizing it into more manageable "chunks." For example, a social security number, which consists of nine pieces of information, can be more easily recalled when chunked in the traditional three sections: xxx - xx - xxxx. Then, one need only recall three pieces of information - the individual chunks - rather than nine separate pieces of information. Three pieces of information are well within the limits of primary memory to hold for rehearsal and transfer to secondary store. This technique thus attempts to "fool" primary memory into exceeding its natural capacity by putting several pieces of information into one.

Our training participants have found this technique quite beneficial. Many of them had never been able to remember their social security number, and found this technique helpful in doing so. This technique has also been used by our participants to remember license plate numbers, drivers license numbers, bank account numbers, and phone numbers. Those reporting the most success with this technique tended to carry the chunking one step further by forming some association with the individual chunks to aid in recall. For example, one participant was trying to recall her friend's new phone number. She had chunked the number into three pieces - the prefix and then two chunks containing the numbers 41 and 69 respectively. She had little trouble remembering the prefix, for it was a common prefix used in the area for years. Remembering the last four numbers was the trick. After breaking it into chunks, she jokingly remarked that her friend maintained that she was 41, but looked more like she was 69. After rehearsing this a few times, she had no trouble recalling her friend's new phone number. Another elaboration strategy reported by some participants involved methods such as examining the mathematical relationships of the different chunks, some of which resulted in quite complicated formulas that would be computed to retrieve the information. A simple illustration is remembering a telephone extension of 5611. This was remembered by breaking it down into two chunks, 56 and 11, and then noticing that when 5 and 6 are added together, they equal 11. Remembering the formula $5 + 6 = 11$ would then provide retrieval of the telephone extension.

These examples of how people have incorporated the use of this technique illustrate nicely how this technique works. In performing the functions of chunking, rehearsal, and elaboration, the information is not only being organized, but also meaning is being applied to the material which will serve as a memory cue. Chunking allows the information to be held in primary store long enough to be "processed" by rehearsal to insure transfer into secondary memory store. The elaboration of the chunks of information provides a cue for recall that will provide easier access to the stored information.

IMAGERY TECHNIQUES

The Method of Loci. The method of loci organizes lists to be remembered by associating them with a well-rehearsed series of locations. An idiographic list of 10 to 20 geographical locations is developed that is used to form visual associations. These locations are typically selected by having individuals take a mental trip through their residence and pick out the desired number of locations. These locations could be pieces of furniture, appliances, rooms, and so on, but should be in the sequential order that would be encountered on an actual walk through the residence. If a list of several items is to be remembered, the first item is visually associated with the first location, the second item with the second location, and so forth. To recall the items, one has merely to mentally walk through each of the locations, which serve as a memory cue for the item associated there. Once recall of a list is no longer required, the associations are forgotten, and a new list can be used with the same locations. Thus, the locations need only be learned once, and they then serve as a "mental chalkboard" where lists can be "written and erased" as needed.

An illustration of this method involves using a short list of five locations to remember a list of five errands to be done tomorrow. The locations in this example come from the kitchen. The tour of the kitchen starts to the right when entering the room, and proceeds in a counterclockwise direction. The first five locations in the kitchen are the refrigerator, stove top, oven, kitchen sink, and garbage disposal. The list of errands to remember tomorrow includes going by the phone company to pay the bill, going to a doctor's appointment, stopping by the grocery store, making a deposit at the bank, and taking the cat to the vet for shots.

Remembering this list of errands involves three steps. The first is to come up with a concrete object to represent the task that is to be performed. This object will serve as a memory cue for the task to be performed. For example, the first errand is to pay the phone bill. One might choose the telephone as the object to use as the memory cue. The next step is to place the object mentally in the first location - the refrigerator. The final step is to spend a few seconds making an association between the refrigerator and the telephone. To make the image stronger, there should be a component of action in the image (Bower, 1970), and a verbal elaboration of the image should be made (Yesavage, Rose, & Bower, 1983). For example, one might form a mental picture of opening up the refrigerator and seeing nothing there except a telephone sitting on the middle shelf. The verbal elaboration could involve thinking how silly it is that the phone is in the refrigerator, and that it would be awfully hard to hear it ringing in there with the door closed.

This procedure is then repeated for the remaining items on the list, placing a reminder object in the location that is next on the walk through the kitchen. To remember the doctor's appointment, one might form an image of a stethoscope boiling in a pot on top of the stove, and think about how hot it would feel if the doctor placed it against one's chest. To remember the trip to the grocery store, an image of opening the oven door and finding a shopping cart stuffed inside, and thinking about how hard it must have been to maneuver it into such a tight spot could serve as an appropriate cue. The trip to the bank to make a deposit could be remembered by an image of the kitchen sink being filled with money, and laughing about how appropriate the image seems since money seems to go down the drain anyway. Taking the cat to the vet could be remembered by creating an image of poor kitty being stuffed down the garbage disposal, the fifth location on the list, and thinking that if the cat really were to be in such a spot, it would really be in need of a trip to the vet.

To recall the list of errands the following morning, one needs merely to take a mental tour of the kitchen, discover the memory cues that were associated there, and recall the tasks for the day. Starting out at the first location - the refrigerator - one recalls the image of opening the door and seeing a phone there. This cue is a reminder to pay the phone bill today. The next location - the stove top - conjures up the image of the stethoscope cooking on the stove, and serves as a reminder of the doctor's appointment. A continued trip through the remaining locations reveals each subsequent memory cue that will serve as a reminder of what needs to be accomplished next.

The nice thing about this technique is that the list is accessible; at any time one can take a mental tour and check what needs to be done next. In addition, if something new comes up during the day that needs to be remembered, a new memory cue can always be placed in the next available location to serve as a reminder to do it later in the day. We typically have participants create a list of 10 locations, which seems to meet most people's needs. If people find themselves needing to remember more than 10 things on a regular basis, however, they can simply expand their list of locations to suit their needs. Some participants have created more than one list - one to remember personal tasks that they must take care of and another to remember job-related tasks.

Research has found that although they require a longer time for retrieval, older adults tend to be as capable of effectively using imagery as younger adults (Treat & Reese, 1976). Robertson-Tchabo et al. (1976) found that older adults significantly improved their recall of a list of 16 nouns using the method of loci with 16 locations. However, their subjects failed to use the technique in a free recall task unless specifically instructed to do so. Robertson-Tchabo et al. (1976) concluded that the method of loci improves organization at the time of encoding and provides retrieval cues to direct the search at the time of recall. This study points out, however, that attention needs to be given to the situations in which this technique can be used, and older adults need to be encouraged to make this technique part of their list of memory strategy techniques.

Participants in our memory training programs tended to find this technique cumbersome as well as rather bizarre. It took a great deal of encouragement to get many of them to give it serious consideration as something that they could incorporate into their daily lives. One of the problems is that it initially takes a good deal of effort to create and remember the list of locations. Secondly, it is initially time-consuming to come up with the concrete images and make the associations needed to use the technique. Those who did use the technique consistently, however, found that these problems soon disappeared. After being used for a few days, the locations became second nature and were easily remembered. In addition, with practice, creating images became much easier and less time-consuming. Participants who used this technique soon found that a list could be effectively encoded in little more time than it took to write the list down. Participants have found it useful for remembering things such as lists of things to do and for shopping lists that do not fit well into categories, and therefore do not lend themselves to categorization.

One participant used this method to memorize a speech that he was to give. He broke his speech down into parts, developed concrete images to represent that part of the speech, and then placed them in his locations. When giving his speech, he took a mental tour of his locations to recall the flow of his talk, and reported getting through the speech without the use of notes. Interestingly, the development of the method of loci is attributed to Roman orators who used the technique to memorize the different parts of a speech, much like our participant (Lapp, 1987).

Because of the effectiveness and utility of this technique, it may be worthwhile to persuade clients to set aside their initial skepticism and encourage them to give it a try. Our experience has been that once mastered, the method of loci is very effective and instills a sense of mastery that is matched by few of the other techniques that are available.

Novel Interacting Images. Novel interacting images is a mnemonic device used to aid in the recall of names, which is the number one memory complaint among older adults (Zelinski et al., 1980). The procedure for this technique is as follows: (a) identify a dominant facial feature of the person whose name is to be remembered, (b) create a concrete visual image from the meaning of the person's name, and (c) form a visual association of the dominant facial feature and the image derived from the name. Recalling the name involves attending to the dominant feature of the face the next time the person is encountered, using that feature as a cue to recall the association made, and decoding the name from that association (McCarty, 1980). This technique will be illustrated by attempting to remember the name of a man just met at a gathering - Mr. Ashburn.

The most important point to keep in mind is that if his name is to be remembered, it is vital that Mr. Ashburn's name is clearly understood when he is introduced. If one is preoccupied with nervousness about meeting someone new or thinking about what to say after the introduction, the name may be missed altogether. In addition, frequently the name is initially given in a way that is not understood, perhaps because the person conducting the introduction is mumbling or talking too fast. One therefore must not be embarrassed to ask for the name to be repeated should it not be understood the first time around. It is surprising how often the failure to remember names is the result of never actually getting the name in the first place. Consequently, in training participants for better name recall, it is stressed that the first and perhaps most important step is getting the name.

Immediately upon approaching Mr. Ashburn to be introduced, the first step in the technique of novel interacting images - identifying his dominant feature - can be accomplished. Ideally, the dominant characteristic should be sought on his face, because that is a characteristic likely to remain constant, as opposed to his clothes or glasses that he may not be wearing the next time he is seen. A good approach here is to notice the first thing that stands out about Mr. Ashburn, and select that as the dominant feature since it is likely to stand out again the next time he is seen. For the purpose of this illustration, it will be assumed that Mr. Ashburn's most striking feature is his very large nose.

The second step in this technique is to transform his name into a concrete image to use as a memory cue to be associated with his dominant feature. Some names lend themselves easily to transformations. A saw or hammer can be used as a cue for the name Carpenter, or a loaf of bread can serve as a cue for the name Baker. Other names, however, present more of a challenge. Ashburn, for example, does not lend itself to a direct transformation. Therefore, an indirect approach based on semantic similarities must be used. This involves breaking the name down into its syllables and using a phonetic approximation to develop a concrete image. The name Herrington, for example, could be broken down into "herring" and "ton," and an image of a ton of herring in a big pile could be created. The name Reagan could be broken down into "Ray" and "gun," and an image of a ray-gun could be used. In this example, Ashburn will be broken down into "ash" and "burn," and an image of a smoldering pile of ashes that is still burning will serve as the concrete image. Some names present quite a challenge in coming up with a concrete image, but we have yet to encounter one that is impossible after some practice and using a little imagination.

The third step in remembering Mr. Ashburn's name is to make an association between the concrete image and the dominant feature that was selected. In this example, one might create the image of a pile of burning ashes sitting on the tip of Mr. Ashburn's large nose. As with the method of loci, the addition of an element of action - perhaps a vision of throwing water on his nose to douse the flames - and a verbal elaboration - thinking that maybe it ought to burn awhile to take off some of the excess - will make the image more memorable.

The recall of Mr. Ashburn's name the next time he is encountered would go something like this: upon meeting, his dominant feature (his large nose) draws attention. Recognition of his dominant feature triggers the image that is associated with it - the burning pile of ashes sitting on the end of it. From that image, the name is reconstructed by decoding the association to produce the name Ashburn which can then be used when he is greeted.

McCarty (1980) performed some of the initial research examining the effectiveness of this technique. He demonstrated the effectiveness of this technique with groups of younger adults, and found that the most difficult aspect of the technique was remembering the association made between the image and the dominant feature, suggesting the importance of the verbal elaboration of the association. In a study with older adults, Yesavage, Rose, and Bower (1983) found that verbally elaborating on a visual image by making an affective judgment about how the image made the participant feel led to greater recall than was achieved by a group that just made the visual image without such elaboration. In addition, it has been found that this technique is more effective when accompanied by pretraining in imagery through tasks such as imagining vivid scenes from poems and literature, studying and reviewing from memory detailed pictures of paintings or line drawings, mental rotation of three-dimensional objects, and exercises based on "find-the-mistake problems" in which subjects were asked to find mistakes in pictures that were slightly altered from a stimulus scene (Yesavage, 1983). Furthermore, older adults with high scores on trait anxiety scales have been found to benefit from relaxation training in using this technique (Yesavage, 1984). Although not yet present in the literature, it is possible that this sort of pretraining in imagery and relaxation training would also be beneficial in using other imagery techniques such as the method of loci.

As with the method of loci, our training participants demonstrated some initial resistance to incorporating this technique for remembering names and faces. The resistance was somewhat easier to overcome, however, because virtually all of them complained of difficulty in remembering people's names, and complained of the embarrassment they experienced with this type of memory lapse. Common complaints about this technique included the time involved in creating images and making associations, difficulty in identifying dominant features, and skepticism about the utility of the technique. As with the method of loci, those participants who practiced reported becoming very efficient in using this technique, and found it extremely helpful in remembering names. Those who seemed to have the most success with the technique initially made a game out of the procedures, attempting to identify dominant features of strangers on the street or faces seen on television. Once these skills were rehearsed, the technique became easy to use, and some participants reported being able to remember quite a few names of new acquaintances met at social gatherings. Like the other techniques, it appears that practice is the key to effectively incorporating this mnemonic strategy into everyday situations.

PHYSICAL REMINDERS

Physical reminders represent the easiest of the memory techniques to use, primarily because most people already use them in some aspect of their lives. Some common examples of physical reminders include the buzzer heard upon entering the car that serves as a reminder to buckle up, the kitchen timer that helps prevent the burning of food, and the buzzer on the dryer that signals the end of the drying cycle so that clothes may be taken out and folded before they get wrinkled. Physical reminders are not actually mnemonic devices in the strict sense of the word; rather, they are ways to manipulate the environment so that instead of trying to remember something, the environment can be arranged to automatically provide reminders. In our training program, we discuss three types of physical reminders: writing things down, placing reminder objects in a prominent place, and associating objects with an established location.

Writing Things Down. Suggesting that someone write something down in order to remember it seems rather pedestrian; it is probably overlooked as an approach to solving memory problems for fear of stating the obvious. It is surprising, however, how seldom people actually use this strategy. For those who are not already doing so, this technique can help enormously in overcoming some of the most common memory concerns such as forgetting appointments, phone numbers, lists of errands to run, dates, and what one had gone to the store to buy.

We focus on three areas: (a) making lists for trips to the store, errands, appointments, and so on, (b) keeping a calendar or monthly reminder book to track upcoming events like sending a birthday card to a friend or doctor appointments scheduled some time ago, and (c) writing notes to serve as reminders for important things to do such as remembering to call the plumber to fix the leaky pipe in the basement. Helping older adults get into the habit of writing things down as a memory aid seems to help in two ways. First, it assists in becoming organized. We urge them to carry a note pad with them to jot things down, and then transfer pertinent information to their monthly planner. Along with the increased organization comes a second benefit, which is a sense of mastery over the minor memory lapses that this technique can help eliminate.

One of the problems run into with this strategy is that although people tend to do a good job at writing notes and lists, these reminders either end up getting left all over the place or are so bunched up on the bulletin board they never get read. A note reminding you to do something 2 days ago is not a very useful memory cue. This brings up the second physical reminder technique - placing reminder objects in a prominent place.

Placing Reminder Objects in a Prominent Place. Notes and calendars can only help if they are looked at. Writing a note to take out the garbage in the morning will not do much good if the note is put in the kitchen drawer where it is not likely to be seen in the morning. If, however, the note is taped to the bathroom mirror where it is sure to be seen in the morning, there is a much better chance of the note serving as a reminder to carry out the garbage. Likewise, one will be more likely to remember to check one's appointment calendar if it is placed in a prominent location such as next to a wallet or purse which is sure to be encountered in the morning. When the wallet or purse is retrieved to carry for the day, there is the calendar next to it serving as a reminder to check it for upcoming appointments, errands, and so on.

Putting other objects in a prominent place can also serve as effective memory cues. One of our training participants got into the habit of placing objects by the door that she needed to take with her when she left the house. For example, if the weather forecast indicated a chance of rain the following day, she would place her umbrella next to the door while she was thinking about it, so that it was sitting there the next morning as a reminder to take it along. Another training participant frequently forgot to turn off her car headlights when conditions were such that she had to turn them on during the daytime. Her solution was to hang a prominent note from her radio knob on the dashboard any time she turned on her lights in the daytime. The note served as a constant reminder that her headlights were on, and solved her problem of forgetting to turn them off when she left the car.

Other examples of placing reminder objects in prominent locations include taking the vacuum cleaner out of the closet and placing it where it can be seen as a reminder to vacuum the house, leaving an empty cereal box on the kitchen counter as a reminder to add that item to the grocery list when you make it up later, and putting your umbrella inside the sleeve of your coat at the restaurant to insure that it will not be forgotten when you leave. The only limits to using this strategy are the limits of the imagination, but with a little of that, the environment can be set up to provide memory cues for a wide variety of situations.

Use of Established Locations. The last physical reminder we discuss is the use of established locations as memory cues. This strategy is applicable for the common complaints of being absentminded; for example, never being able to find the car keys, or forgetting where shoes were taken off and left. The technique is very simple - first, one makes a list of those items that are frequently misplaced. Next, an obvious, familiar location for each item is selected. Finally, a habit is developed of placing those items only in their chosen location. The hardest part about this technique is developing the habit of putting things in their assigned location. Once that is accomplished, however, this technique works very well. One of our training participants complained that she would hide presents for her grandchildren, money, and other items, but would then have trouble remembering where she hid them when it came time to retrieve them. Her solution was to designate three different hiding places in her house, one of which she would use when she wanted to hide something. When it came time to get the item, she then knew that it would be in one of three places, making her search for the item much less frustrating.

The usefulness of these physical reminders as memory cues cannot be overstated. The beauty of these strategies is that they take very little effort to use, yet they can compensate for many of the everyday lapses in memory that older (and younger) adults experience. Training participants were initially encouraged to use these techniques by our giving homework assignments, for example, "Bring in to our next session three examples of how you used placing an object in a prominent location as a memory cue." As participants discussed and shared the myriad imaginative applications of these techniques, they quickly realized that these simple methods greatly reduced the occurrence of many embarrassing memory lapses, and greatly facilitated their sense of mastery over their ability to remember things.

All of the memory techniques discussed above - chunking, categorization, the method of loci, novel interacting images, and physical reminders - provide ways to improve the efficiency of storing and retrieving information, and serve to decrease the occurrence of memory failures. It would not be realistic, however, to think that each of these techniques will be beneficial for everyone. We have encountered participants in our training programs that absolutely refuse to use the imagery techniques, and others who found that the physical reminders take care of most of their needs and therefore did not bother using the other ones that take much more "mental energy" to incorporate.

One of the delightful aspects of providing this training to older adults has been seeing participants take these techniques and alter, modify, and even bastardize them into idiographic strategies that could work only for them. These techniques do not need to be followed exactly. This is especially true of the imagery techniques which can be very effective even if only a portion of the technique is used. A good example is novel interacting images for remembering names. Very few of our participants use this technique by the letter, but most have learned that if you make some type of an association with the name, you are much more likely to remember it. Embedded within these techniques are the clues for how we remember things. It is these clues that we as trainers and therapists have to offer those with whom we work; how these clues are interpreted and incorporated into the lives of those we train is the responsibility of the trainees. Originality and experimentation should be encouraged with these strategies, for the bottom line is that if it works for them, it works.

SETTING

Memory training programs for older adults have traditionally been offered in university, community agency, or hospital settings. Most often these programs are groups led by one or more trainers; these groups are relatively short in duration (4 to 5 weeks) and are offered as a community service (i.e., free of charge). This book focuses on the uses of memory training as a component of a multimodal intervention program for older adults. Consider an example. A 71-year-old woman is referred to a clinical psychologist by her physician. The client's presenting problems are depressed mood, loneliness, and difficulties in her relationship with her daughter. Upon greater inquiry, it is discovered that she also feels that her memory is poor and failing.

As is so often the case in work with older adults, this hypothetical case calls for an eclectic, multimodal intervention. Of course, one component we would argue for is a program for her memory complaints. At what point memory training would be offered in the course of her treatment is a clinical decision, though in the present case it would probably follow attention to the more pressing concerns of depression and family discord. Memory training would not be offered as a separate treatment, but would instead be integrated into a comprehensive treatment plan. For example, treatment with the hypothetical 71-year-old depressed client might have first focused on issues related to her depression, such as self-criticalness, inactivity, and misattributions. It would be quite likely that such a client would also hold dysfunctional beliefs about memory functioning. If the client responded favorably to this depression treatment approach, then it might be extended to her beliefs about her memory functioning. The practitioner might examine questions of this sort: Does the client magnify memory failures and minimize memory successes? Does she expect more of her memory functioning than is reasonable? Are memory lapses interpreted as personal failures?

The other major component of the memory intervention would be mnemonic training. This too could be merged with the ongoing treatment plan. The point is that memory training can readily be included as a component of comprehensive clinical interventions for older adults. Furthermore, provision of memory training need not be reserved for specialists such as neuropsychologists or clinical geropsychologists. With a modest amount of preparation, a practitioner should be ready to assist an older client concerned with his or her memory function.

APPLICATIONS

A thorough assessment should yield sufficient information for planning a specific memory training program. In a typical research program, clients with a variety of memory complaint, memory performance, and affective disturbance typologies are entered into uniform training conditions. Clinically, this is probably not the optimal approach. Presumably, practitioners will be able to individually tailor a training program for their client. Our attention is now turned to what might constitute such a program.

For clients with a memory performance deficit, instruction in mnemonic strategies is the suggested intervention. Such instruction is enhanced if clients are given an overview of the presumed processes of encoding, storage, and retrieval and the effects of aging on these processes. Giving a rationale for the effort they will be asked to expend in learning new skills appears to be an important ingredient for success. If a client's memory complaints are diffuse, instruction may be provided in all of the validated techniques reviewed previously (chunking, categorization, novel interacting images, method of loci, and the use of physical reminders). The practitioner wishing more information on these techniques than what is presented herein will find presentations of them in self-help books by Lorayne and Lucas (1974), Scogin and Flynn (1986), and Lapp (1987). Experience suggests that most older adults will have diffuse, global memory complaints (e.g., "I just don't remember things as well as I used to").

Some clients will present with a specific memory complaint. For example, difficulty in remembering names is a frequent complaint for all age groups. Following an overview of memory and aging, this client might be offered instruction in novel interacting images, a technique designed to improve name recall. To continue with this hypothetical client, one might augment instruction in novel interacting images with relaxation training (Yesavage, 1984) and imagery exercises (Yesavage, Rose, & Bower, 1983). As mentioned earlier, these additional components have been shown to improve acquisition of the mnemonic, enhance recall, and sustain improvement at follow-up. Homework assignments could be constructed from the self-help books mentioned earlier; these books would also provide the practitioner with exercises and practice material for in-session training. Practitioners may also choose to make the memory training self-taught by providing the client with one of the self-help books and discussing progress during individual treatment sessions.

If, following assessment, it appears that attention needs to be devoted to the client's level or intensity of memory complaint, then procedures in addition to mnemonic instruction would be indicated. The suggested intervention would be an adaptation of cognitive therapy principles to memory concerns. Elliott and Lachman (1989) have made similar recommendations for combining memory training with modification of control beliefs, attributions, and performance goals by cognitive restructuring. Practitioners unfamiliar with cognitive therapy are referred to Beck et al. (1979) for general coverage and Thompson et al. (1986) for applications to older adults.

Cognitive therapy has been shown to be an effective treatment for geriatric depression (e.g., Beutler et al., 1987; Thompson, Gallagher, & Breckenridge, 1987), and the extension of this modality to the memory training area seems well suited for several reasons. Memory complaints and depression are highly associated. An older adult with substantial memory complaint is also likely to experience some level of affective disturbance. Furthermore, memory complaints have been shown to be attitudinal in nature, and consequently not easily changed as the result of modest improvements in memory function resulting from memory training. One of the premises of cognitive therapy is that the therapist and client engage in collaborative empiricism. Examining older adults' beliefs about their memory functioning in an empirical fashion is a likely extension of cognitive therapy to memory training. Clients could also be taught to monitor their thoughts and attributions following memory tasks, especially failures, and guided to more adaptive cognitions.

There are a couple of ways in which to augment memory training with cognitive therapy principles. The first, and more traditional, is through one-to-one consultation. For more directive service providers, a segment of one or more sessions could be devoted to exploring an aspect of cognitive therapy such as automatic thoughts or one of the cognitive errors. A manual for cognitive therapy with older adults is available for guidance (Yost et al., 1986).

Another option for providing the cognitive therapy component is through bibliotherapy, or directed reading. Bibliotherapy for depressed older adults has demonstrated efficacy (Scogin, Hamblin, & Beutler, 1987). We recommend *Feeling Good* by David Burns (1980). The advantage of bibliotherapy is that it is cost- and time-efficient and allows the practitioner to devote more time to instruction in mnemonic usage. Homework assignments can be made from the book and review of assignments conducted during sessions.

In this multimodal approach that we advocate, other efficacious interventions, such as exercise and nutrition, could be blended into the programs based on the practitioner's knowledge and client's receptivity. We do caution that memory training components should be proven to be efficacious prior to delivery. Memory training is frequently associated with the advertisements seen in the back pages of magazines promising "Perfect Memory" or "Total Recall" or some other preposterous claim; practitioners should be judicious in their service provision.

RESEARCH ON MEMORY TRAINING PROGRAMS

Several authors have applied the techniques discussed previously in group training settings (Yesavage, 1983; Yesavage, Rose, & Bower, 1983; Zarit, Cole, & Guider, 1981; Zarit, Gallagher, & Kramer, 1981). Zarit, Gallagher, and Kramer (1981) compared group memory training consisting of instruction on specific memory strategies with a group receiving problem-solving skills, assertiveness training, and other self-growth topics. These investigators examined the effects of these group approaches on both memory complaints and memory performance. Although the memory training group significantly improved in performance on tasks requiring categorization and visual mediation immediately following training, follow-up testing revealed no significant differences between groups on these tasks. It was interesting that a significant reduction in subjective memory concerns was seen in both groups. These changes were most highly correlated with improvements in affective status which occurred over the course of the groups. These findings point to the higher correlation between affective status and memory complaints and the lower correlation between memory complaints and actual memory performance.

In another study, Zarit, Cole, and Guider (1981) compared the effects of a memory training group, a current events group, and a wait list group on memory complaints, memory performance, and affective status. It was found that subjects in the memory training group significantly improved their performance on tasks requiring organization of information into categories and visual imagery. As in the previous study, subjects in both the training group and the discussion group displayed a decrease in memory complaints by the end of the study, but these results were not associated with a corresponding improvement in affective status. In comparison to a waiting list group, memory training resulted in a significant improvement in memory performance over the wait list group in all areas except recognition tasks, on which both groups performed highly during pretesting. Memory complaints decreased significantly for subjects in the training group, while they increased slightly in the wait list group. Therefore, the benefit of memory training was improved memory performance, but subjective appraisals of memory were again not related to memory performance. It would therefore appear that merely participating in a group can be sufficient to lower subjective memory complaints.

Memory training has also been applied through a self-taught program (Scogin et al., 1985). Sixty participants were randomly assigned to either self-taught memory training or a delayed training control group. Participants were assessed on measures of objective and subjective memory functioning and depression. Participants assigned to memory training were given a manual containing information about memory changes that occur with aging, instruction in various memory strategies, and numerous memory exercises to be completed on a daily basis while working on the program. The memory program was designed to be completed in 16 days, though trainees were given up to 4 weeks to complete the training. While working on the manual, participants were contacted weekly by research assistants to monitor progress and answer questions about the training. The results suggested that this approach led to improved memory performance on some but not all measures, and these improvements were maintained at a 1-month follow-up.

A second aspect of this research compared the subjective and objective memory functioning of the memory training participants (high-complaint group) to a similar group of older adults who had not requested memory training (low-complaint group). The groups were predictably different in their subjective memory functioning reports, with training participants rating their memory as poorer. However, on measures of objective memory functioning, such as free recall and name-face learning, the groups were quite comparable. These findings suggest that the subjective aspects of functioning are quite important in the design of memory training programs.

Research on self-taught memory training was extended in a recent investigation (Scogin & Prohaska, 1992). The self-taught memory training program was compared to attention-placebo and delayed training control groups. Sixty-nine adults 60 years of age and older were randomly placed into the three groups. Participants were community-dwelling elders and free of serious cognitive impairment as evidenced by screening with the Mental Status Questionnaire (Kahn et al., 1960). The attention-placebo training consisted of reading a book on time management. Both the memory training and attention-placebo groups were superior to the control group in terms of memory performance improvement, but the memory training and attention-placebo groups were equally effective. Based on this finding, one would find little to recommend in the self-taught memory training program, but, fortunately, improvements in subjective memory functioning were superior for the memory training participants. More specifically, participants who received memory training felt that their memory capacity had increased following training. This is a potentially important finding, because concerns about memory functioning, not necessarily actual memory performance decrements, are what motivate older adults to participate in memory training. A provocative finding in this study was that significant others (e.g., spouse, child, friend) observed a decrease in the frequency of memory problems experienced by participants. These findings await replication but do generally suggest that the major impact of memory training may be in the subjective memory performance domain.

There are other skills that may augment the effectiveness of memory training. As previously mentioned, Yesavage (1984) found that relaxation training improved the ability of older adults to use a mnemonic device and improved recall. Yesavage (1983) also found that pretraining in imagery improved the ability of older adults to use imagery-based mnemonic devices. One limitation to the existing research is that there has been little long-term follow-up to indicate whether these techniques are generalized and incorporated into the everyday lives of those learning them. In a 3-year follow-up study, Scogin and Bienias (1988) found that subjects who had received memory training were performing at levels comparable to those at pretraining. Memory complaints had likewise remained unchanged from pretraining levels. In addition, only 28% of the participants in the follow-up study reported using the mnemonic devices. This suggests that more efforts at generalization during training may be necessary if the techniques are to be truly useful in day-to-day functioning.

CONSIDERATIONS AND PROBLEMS

Lest memory training seem simpler than it really is, we will mention some of the issues encountered in offering this form of intervention. First are the qualifications of the service provider. Credentials per se are less important than knowledge in some particular areas. Especially relevant is some familiarity with the area of memory and aging, especially the dementing illnesses. It is almost assured that in the course of providing services for older adults with memory complaints, the topic of Alzheimer's disease will be broached. One does not need training as a neurologist or neuropsychologist to provide useful information and support to the client concerned about this ominous disease. It is also important that one be prepared to make referral to a specialist for further evaluation if the client's memory impairments are beginning to adversely affect his or her functioning.

What about motivation? Typical clients are motivated to engage in a memory enhancement program, but this is not always the case. For example, in our research studies some participants come to training under coercion from family. The motivation for the required practice and rehearsal is not usually present for such participants. Memory training does take some work, so client motivation is a prerequisite. Thus, clients wanting effortless memory improvement will not find it in what has been discussed herein. This point should be made prior to initiating training.

Two additional concerns are compliance and maintenance. In our research programs, compliance has been quite high. However, work with individual older adults may result in more problematic compliance issues. Frequent assessment and monitoring of progress as an antidote to noncompliance is recommended. As noted earlier, memory training is relatively hard work, so that the experience of progress is important to continued motivation. These assessments could parallel and perhaps duplicate the measures given before training, including objective and subjective memory functioning tasks.

Assessment of the client's memory functioning also allows the practitioner to evaluate the utility of training components and identify problem areas needing further attention. For example, one might be focusing on improved performance on name-face recall and in the course of reassessment discover that the client is performing the novel interacting images technique correctly except for the step involving concentration on a prominent facial feature. With this information, the practitioner could focus on this aspect of the mnemonic.

Maintenance of training effects is also a concern. Most of the research conducted on memory training suggests that training effects are fairly well maintained over 1- to 2-month intervals. Sheikh, Hill, and Yesavage (1986) found maintenance of training at 6-month follow-up, however, Scogin and Bienias (1988) found little evidence of durability of memory training at a 3-year follow-up. We are currently evaluating effects of booster review sessions in which participants return at 3 months following the end of training. We anticipate that such booster sessions will encourage participants to review the training and will provide some encouragement for their continued application of the techniques. These sessions may be face-to-face or via the telephone for community-dwelling older adults and would most logically include both a review of the training offered and a discussion of applications of the techniques made by the client in the period following training.

SUMMARY AND CONCLUSIONS

Older adults will almost certainly comprise an increasing share of practitioners' case loads. One of the more frequent complaints of older adults concerns their memory functioning. For this reason, service providers should be aware of the research relating to memory and aging, and the efficacy of different types of memory training. A brief summary of this literature follows. First, age-associated memory impairment is primarily concentrated in secondary and effortful memory processes. Second, the level and intensity of memory complaints are not necessarily indicative of the degree of memory impairment. This lack of correspondence between complaint and performance is especially likely in depressed clients. Third, memory training programs have demonstrated modest efficacy in improving memory performance. We advocate the extension of these programs into multimodal, comprehensive treatment programs for older adults.

Assessment of the older client's memory complaints and memory performance is necessary prior to training. Targets for intervention should present themselves following assessment. Mnemonic strategies exist for many of the complaints frequently made by older clients - such as name recall and reading retention. Mnemonic instruction augmented with relaxation training and imagery rehearsal has added benefits for the older client. Because depression and memory complaints have been shown to be highly correlated, therapeutic techniques that have been shown to reduce depression, such as cognitive therapy, should also prove beneficial. The use of booster sessions following training in order to facilitate generalization and maintenance is also advocated.

The limitations of memory training are, unfortunately, rather numerous. At best, the effects of extant memory training programs are modest. Dramatic changes in objective memory functioning do not occur. Not only are the effects modest, but the motivation of the client must be high in order to realize modest improvements. The types of techniques presented in this document generally require considerable diligence to acquire and apply. Furthermore, persistence is required to maintain skill in the application of memory enhancement techniques. Yet another limitation of memory training concerns the relevance of mnemonic strategies such as the method of loci and novel interacting images to the everyday memory concerns of older adults. These limitations suggest directions for clinical research. The most formidable research would involve development of more powerful memory-enhancing techniques and environments. Interventions that produced more demonstrative effects would most probably result in greater client motivation and persistence. Additional research is needed to explore the optimization of outcome by matching intervention foci to the needs of the client. For example, it is logical to assume that a client evidencing mild depression, high memory complaints, and average memory performance would profit most from a training program that addresses the affective components in concert with memory enhancement training. However, specifically tailored programs of this sort have not been empirically evaluated. Matching of client needs to intervention strategy may accelerate memory training from a modest to a moderate impact therapy.

Treating memory complaints among older adults may seem to be a highly specialized endeavor. However, we believe and hope we have conveyed that provision of memory training need not be reserved only for those with specialized interests and/or training. With the likely increase in demand for services by older adults, practitioners will be better able to meet the needs of their clientele if memory training techniques are added to their armamentarium.

REFERENCES

American Psychiatric Association. (1987). *Diagnostic and Statistical Manual of Mental Disorders* (3rd ed. rev.). Washington, DC: Author.

Beck, A. T., Rush, A. J., Shaw, B. F., & Emery, G. (1979). *Cognitive Therapy of Depression*. New York: Guilford.

Beck, A. T., Ward, C. H., Mendelson, M., Mock, J., & Erbaugh, J. (1961). An inventory for measuring depression. *Archives of General Psychiatry, 4,* 561-571.

Beutler, L. E., Scogin, F., Kirkish, P., Schretlen, D., Corbishley, A., Hamblin, D., Meredith, K., Potter, R., Bamford, C. R., & Levenson, A. I. (1987). Group cognitive therapy and alprazolam in the treatment of depression in older adults. *Journal of Consulting and Clinical Psychology, 55,* 550-556.

Bower, G. H. (1970). Analysis of a mnemonic device. *American Scientist, 58,* 496-510.

Burns, D. (1980). *Feeling Good.* New York: Guilford.

Buschke, H. (1984). Control of cognitive processing. In L. R. Squire & N. Butters (Eds.), *Neuropsychology of Memory* (pp. 33-40). New York: Guilford.

Butters, N., Martone, M., White, B., Granholm, E., & Wolfe, J. (1986). Clinical validators: Comparisons of demented and amnestic patients. In L. W. Poon (Ed.), *Handbook for Clinical Memory Assessment of Older Adults* (pp. 337-352). Washington, DC: American Psychological Association.

Camp, C. J., Markley, R. P., & Kramer, J. J. (1983). Spontaneous use of mnemonics by elderly individuals. *Educational Gerontology, 9,* 57-71.

Cerella, J., & Poon, L. W. (1981). Age and parafoveal sensitivity. *The Gerontologist, 12,* 76.

Craik, F. I. M. (1977). Age differences in human memory. In J. E. Birren & K. W. Schaie (Eds.), *Handbook of the Psychology of Aging* (pp. 348-420). New York: Van Nostrand Reinhold.

Crook, T., Bartus, R. T., Ferris, S. H., Whitehouse, P., Cohen, G. D., & Gershon, S. (1986). Age-associated memory impairment: Proposed diagnostic criteria and measures of clinical change-Report of a National Institute of Mental Health work group. *Developmental Neuropsychology, 2,* 261-276.

Derogatis, L. R., Rickels, K., & Rock, A. F. (1976). The SCL-90 and the MMPI: A step in the validation of a new self-report scale. *British Journal of Psychiatry, 128,* 280-289.

Derogatis, L. R., & Spencer, P. M. (1982). *The Brief Symptom Inventory: Administration, Scoring and Procedures.* Baltimore, MD: Clinical Psychometric Research.

Dixon, R. A., & Hultsch, D. F. (1984). The Metamemory in Adulthood (MIA) Instrument. *Psychological Documents, 14,* 3.

Elliott, E., & Lachman, M. E. (1989). Enhancing memory by modifying control beliefs, attributions, and performance goals in the elderly. In P. S. Fry (Ed.), *Psychological Perspective of Helplessness and Control in the Elderly.* North-Holland: Elsevier Science Publishers.

Erber, J. T. (1981). Remote memory and age: A review. *Experimental Aging Research, 1,* 189-199.

Eysenck, M. W. (1974). Age differences in incidental learning. *Developmental Psychology, 10,* 936-941.

Finkel, S. I., & Yesavage, J. A. (1990). Learning mnemonics: A preliminary evaluation of a computer-aided instruction package for the elderly. *Experimental Aging Research, 15,* 199-201.

Folstein, M. F., Folstein, S. E., & McHugh, P. R. (1975). Mini-Mental State: A practical method for grading the cognitive state of the patient for the clinician. *Journal of Psychiatric Research, 12,* 189-198.

Gallagher, D. (1986). Assessment of depression by interview methods and psychiatric rating scales. In L. W. Poon (Ed.), *Handbook for Clinical Memory Assessment of Older Adults* (pp. 202-212). Washington, DC: American Psychological Association.

Gilewski, M. J., & Zelinski, E. M. (1986). Questionnaire assessment of memory complaints. In L. W. Poon (Ed.), *Handbook for Clinical Memory Assessment of Older Adults* (pp. 93-107). Washington, DC: American Psychological Association.

Gilewski, M. J., Zelinski, E. M., & Schaie, K. W. (1990). The memory functioning questionnaire for assessment of memory complaints in adulthood and old age. *Psychology and Aging, 5,* 482-490.

Hamilton, M. (1967). Development of a rating scale for primary depressive illness. *British Journal of Social and Clinical Psychology, 6,* 278-296.

Henry, G. M., Weingartner, H., & Murphy, D. L. (1973). Influence of affective states and psychoactive drugs on verbal learning and memory. *American Journal of Psychiatry, 130,* 966-971.

Hilbert, N. M., Niederehe, G., & Kahn, R. L. (1976). Accuracy and speed of memory in depressed and organic aged. *Educational Gerontology, 1,* 131-146.

Hulicka, I. M., & Grossman, J. L. (1967). Age-group comparisons for the use of mediators in paired-associate learning. *Journal of Gerontology, 22,* 46-51.

Hultsch, D. F., & Dixon, R. A. (1990). Learning and memory in aging. In J. E. Birren & K. W. Schaie (Eds.), *Handbook of the Psychology of Aging* (3rd ed., pp. 259-274). San Diego: Academic Press.

Kahn, R. L., Goldfarb, A. I., Pollack, M., & Peck, A. (1960). Brief objective measures for the determination of mental status in the aged. *American Journal of Psychiatry, 117,* 326-328.

Kahn, R. L., Zarit, S. H., Hilbert, N. M., & Niederehe, G. A. (1975). Memory complaint and impairment in the aged: The effect of depression and altered brain function. *Archives of General Psychiatry, 32,* 1560-1573.

Kaszniak, A. W., Poon, L. W., & Riege, W. (1986). Assessing memory deficits: An information-processing approach. In L. W. Poon (Ed.), *Handbook for Clinical Memory Assessment of Older Adults* (pp. 168-188). Washington, DC: American Psychological Association.

Lapp, D. (1987). *Don't Forget: Easy Exercises for a Better Memory at Any Age.* New York: McGraw-Hill.

Laurence, M. W. (1967). Memory loss with age: A test of two strategies for its retardation. *Psychonomic Science, 9,* 209-210.

Leirer, V. O., Morrow, D. G., Pariante, G. M., & Sheikh, J. I. (1988). Elders' nonadherence, its assessment, and computer assisted instruction for medication recall training. *Journal of the American Geriatrics Society, 36,* 877-884.

Lorayne, H., & Lucas, J. (1974). *The Memory Book.* New York: Ballentine.

Lowenthal, M. F., Berkman, P. L., Buehler, J. A., Pierce, R. C., Robinson, B. C., & Trier, M. L. (1967). *Aging and Mental Disorder in San Francisco.* San Francisco: Jossey Bass.

McCarty, D. L. (1980). Investigation of a visual imagery mnemonic device for acquiring face-name associations. *Journal of Experimental Psychology, 6,* 145-155.

Meier, M. J., Benton, A. L., & Diller, L. (1987). *Neuropsychological Rehabilitation.* New York: Guilford.

Niederehe, G. (1986). Depression and memory impairment in the aged. In L. W. Poon (Ed.), *Handbook for Clinical Memory Assessment of Older Adults* (pp. 226-237). Washington, DC: American Psychological Association.

O'Connor, M., & Cermak, L. S. (1987). Rehabilitation of organic memory disorders. In M. J. Meier, A. L. Benton, & L. Diller (Eds.), *Neuropsychological Rehabilitation* (pp. 260-279). New York: Guilford.

O'Hara, M. W., Hinricks, J. V., Kohout, F. J., Wallace, R. B., & Lemke, J. H. (1986). Memory complaint and memory performance in the depressed elderly. *Psychology and Aging, 1,* 208-214.

Poon, L. W. (1985). Differences in human memory with aging: Nature, causes, and clinical implications. In J. E. Birren & K. W. Schaie (Eds.), *Handbook of the Psychology of Aging* (2nd ed., pp. 427-462). New York: Van Nostrand Reinhold.

Poon, L. W. (Ed.). (1986). *Handbook for Clinical Memory Assessment of Older Adults.* Washington, DC: American Psychological Association.

Popkin, S. J., Gallagher, D., Thompson, L. W., & Moore, M. (1982). Memory complaint and performance in normal and depressed older adults. *Experimental Aging Research, 8,* 141-145.

Rabbitt, P. M. (1964). Grouping of stimuli in pattern recognition as a function of age. *Quarterly Journal of Experimental Psychology, 16,* 172-176.

Robertson-Tchabo, E. A., Hausman, C. P., & Arenberg, D. (1976). A classical mnemonic for older learners: A trip that works! *Educational Gerontology, 1,* 215-226.

Rosen, W. G., Terry, R. D., Fuld, P. A., Katzman, R., & Peck, A. (1980). Pathological verification of ischemic score in differentiation of dementias. *Annals of Neurology, 7,* 486-488.

Salmon, D. P., & Butters, N. (1987). Recent developments in learning and memory: Implications for the rehabilitation of the amnesic patient. In M. J. Meier, A. L. Benton, & L. Diller (Eds.), *Neuropsychological Rehabilitation* (pp. 280-293). New York: Guilford.

Sanders, R. E., Murphy, M. D., Schmitt, F. A., & Walsh, K. K. (1980). Age differences in free recall rehearsal strategies. *Journal of Gerontology, 35,* 550-558.

Schmitt, F. A., Martin, M. D., & Sanders, R. E. (1981). Training older adult free recall rehearsal strategies. *Journal of Gerontology, 36,* 329-337.

Scogin, F. (1985). Memory complaints and memory performance: The relationship reexamined. *Journal of Applied Gerontology, 14,* 79-89.

Scogin, F., & Bienias, J. L. (1988). A three-year follow-up of older adult participants in a memory-skills training program. *Psychology and Aging, 3,* 334-337.

Scogin, F., & Flynn, T. (1986). Manual for memory skills training. *Social and Behavioral Sciences Documents, 16,* 14.

Scogin, F., Hamblin, D., & Beutler, L. (1987). Bibliotherapy for depressed older adults: A self-help alternative. *The Gerontological Society of America, 27,* 383-387.

Scogin, F., & Prohaska, M. (1992). The efficacy of self-taught memory training for community-dwelling older adults. *Educational Gerontology, 18,* 751-766.

Scogin, F., & Rohling, M. (1990). Cognitive processes, self-reports of memory functioning and mental health status in older adults. *Journal of Aging and Health, 1,* 507-520.

Scogin, F., Storandt, M., & Lott, L. (1985). Memory skills training, memory complaints, and depression in older adults. *Journal of Gerontology, 40,* 562-568.

Sheikh, J. I., Hill, R. D., & Yesavage, J. A. (1986). Long-term efficacy of cognitive training for age associated memory impairment: A six-month follow-up study. *Developmental Neuropsychology, 2,* 413-421.

Skilbeck, C. (1984). Computer assistance in the management of memory and cognitive impairment. In B. A. Wilson & N. Moffat (Eds.), *Clinical Management of Memory Problems* (pp. 112-131). Rockville, MD: Aspen.

Spitzer, R. L., & Endicott, J. (1978). *NIMH Clinical Research Branch Collaborative Program on the Psychobiology of Depression: Schedule for Affective Disorders and Schizophrenia (SADS).* New York: New York State Psychiatric Institute, Biometrics Research Division.

Thompson, L. W. (1980). Period "lapses" in attentional processes: A possible correlate of memory impairment in the elderly. In L. W. Poon, J. L. Fozard, L. S. Cermak, D. Arenberg, & L. W. Thompson (Eds.), *New Directions in Memory and Aging: Proceedings of the George Talland Memorial Conference* (pp. 239-242). Hillsdale, NJ: Erlbaum.

Thompson, L. W., Davies, R., Gallagher, D., & Krantz, S. E. (1986). Cognitive therapy with older adults. In T. L. Brink (Ed.), *Clinical Gerontology: A Guide to Assessment and Intervention* (pp. 245-280). New York: Haworth.

Thompson, L. W., Gallagher, D., & Breckenridge, J. S. (1987). Comparative effectiveness of psychotherapies for depressed elders. *Journal of Consulting and Clinical Psychology, 55,* 385-390.

Treat, N. J., & Reese, H. W. (1976). Age, pacing, and imagery in paired-associate learning. *Developmental Psychology, 12,* 119-124.

Wechsler, D. A. (1981). *Wechsler Adult Intelligence Scale - Revised.* New York: The Psychological Corporation.

Wechsler, D. A. (1987). *Wechsler Memory Scale - Revised Manual.* San Diego: The Psychological Corporation.

Wilson, B. A. (1987). *Rehabilitation of Memory.* New York: Guilford.

Yesavage, J. A. (1983). Imagery pre-training and memory training in the elderly. *Gerontology, 29,* 271-275.

Yesavage, J. A. (1984). Relaxation and memory training in 39 elderly patients. *American Journal of Psychiatry, 141,* 778-781.

Yesavage, J. A. (1985). Nonpharmacologic treatments for memory losses with normal aging. *American Journal of Psychiatry, 142,* 600-605.

Yesavage, J. A. (1986). The use of self-rating depression scales in the elderly. In L. W. Poon (Ed.), *Handbook for Clinical Memory Assessment of Older Adults* (pp. 213-217). Washington, DC: American Psychological Association.

Yesavage, J. A., Brink, T. L., Rose, T. S., Lum, O., Huang, U., Adey, M., & Leirer, V. O. (1983). Development and validation of a geriatric screening scale: A preliminary report. *Journal of Psychiatric Research, 17,* 37-49.

Yesavage, J. A., Rose, T. L., & Bower, G. H. (1983). Interactive imagery and affective judgments improve face-name learning in the elderly. *Journal of Gerontology, 38,* 197-203.

Yost, E. B., Beutler, L. E., Corbishley, M. A., & Allender, J. R. (1986). *Group Cognitive Therapy: A Treatment Approach for Depressed Older Adults.* New York: Pergamon.

Zarit, S. H. (1980). *Aging and Mental Disorders: Psychological Approaches to Assessment and Treatment* (pp. 22-48, 184-213). New York: Free Press.

Zarit, S. H., Cole, K. D., & Guider, R. L. (1981). Memory training strategies and subjective complaints of memory in the aged. *The Gerontologist, 21,* 158-165.

Zarit, S. H., Gallagher, D., & Kramer, N. (1981). Memory training in the community aged: Effects of depression, memory complaint, and memory performance. *Educational Gerontology, 6,* 11-27.

Zelinski, E. M., Gilewski, M. J., & Thompson, L. W. (1980). Do laboratory tests relate to self-assessment of memory ability in the young and old? In L. W. Poon, J. L. Fozard, L. S. Cermak, D. Arenberg, & L. W. Thompson (Eds.), *New Directions in Memory and Aging* (pp. 519-544). Hillsdale, NJ: Lawrence Erlbaum.

Other Titles In Our Practitioner's Resource Series

Each of these unique paperbound books focuses on a topic of critical and timely importance. These are concise, practice-oriented guidebooks designed to provide quick access to new concepts and applied clinical techniques.

Price Per Book: $9.95 Each.

Prices and availability subject to change without notice.

See Reverse Side For Ordering Information————————▶

Order Form

Please Send Me The Following Books:

Quantity	Description of Product/Product Code	Price
	SUBTOTAL	
	FLORIDA ORDERS, ADD 7% SALES TAX	
	SHIPPING	
	TOTAL	

SHIPPING CHARGES
Up to $15.99 Order, Add $2.00 in US, $3.25 Foreign
$16 - $30.99 Order, Add $2.75 in US, $4.00 Foreign
$31 - $45.99 Order, Add $3.75 in US, $5.00 Foreign
$46 - $70.99 Order, Add $4.25 in US, $6.00 Foreign
Orders over $71, Add 7% in US, 10% Foreign
Call for charges for 1, 2, or 3 day US delivery or Foreign air

❑   Check or money order enclosed (payable to PRP; US funds only)

Charge my ❑ MasterCard   ❑ Visa   ❑ Discover   ❑ American Express

Signature (Required if using credit card)_____

Card #_____ Expiration Date_____

Ship To:

Name_____
[Please Print]

Address_____

Address_____

City/State/Zip_____

Daytime Phone # (_____)_____

Order From:
Professional Resource Press • P.O. Box 15560 • Sarasota, FL 34277-1560
Telephone # 813-366-7913 • FAX # 813-366-7971

Would You Like Information On Our Other Publications?

For a copy of our latest catalog, please write, call, or fax the following information to the address and phone number listed below:

Name_____
[Please Print]

Address_____

Address_____

City/State/Zip_____

Telephone_____

Profession (check all that apply):

_____ Psychologist   _____ Mental Health Counselor
_____ Marriage and Family Therapist   _____ Psychiatrist
_____ School Psychologist   _____ Not in Mental Health Field
_____ Clinical Social Worker   _____ Other:_____

Professional Resource Press
P.O. Box 15560
Sarasota, FL 34277-1560

Telephone # 813-366-7913
FAX # 813-366-7971